For Daniel
—F.R.

For Sam
—J.D.Z.

Text copyright © 1996 by Fay Robinson.
Illustrations copyright © 1996 by Jean Day Zallinger.
All rights reserved. Published by Scholastic Inc.
Printed in the U.S.A.
ISBN 0-590-06679-X
HELLO READER!, CARTWHEEL BOOKS, and the CARTWHEEL BOOKS logo are registered
trademarks of Scholastic Inc.

5 6 7 8 9 10   23   03 02 01 00 99 98

Great Snakes!

by Fay Robinson
Illustrated by Jean Day Zallinger

Hello Science Reader!

SCHOLASTIC INC. Cartwheel ·B·O·O·K·S·®
New York   Toronto   London   Auckland   Sydney

Two snakes.

Four snakes.

Six snakes.

Eight.

Every single snake is great!

Snakes with diamonds,

stripes,

and dots.

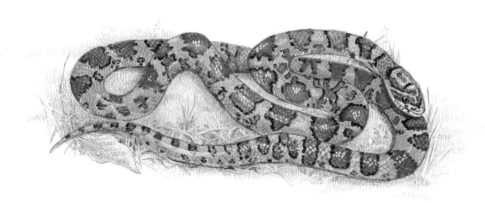

Snakes with many
kinds of spots.

Snakes in deserts.

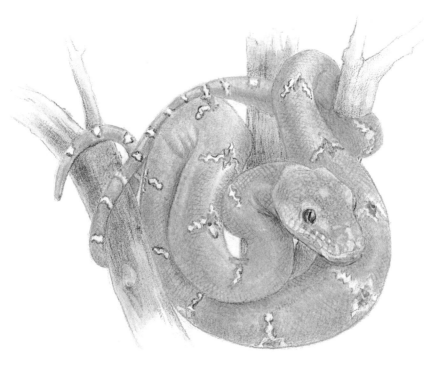

Snakes in trees.

Snakes in mountains.

Snakes in seas.

With no legs,
snakes climb

and slide.

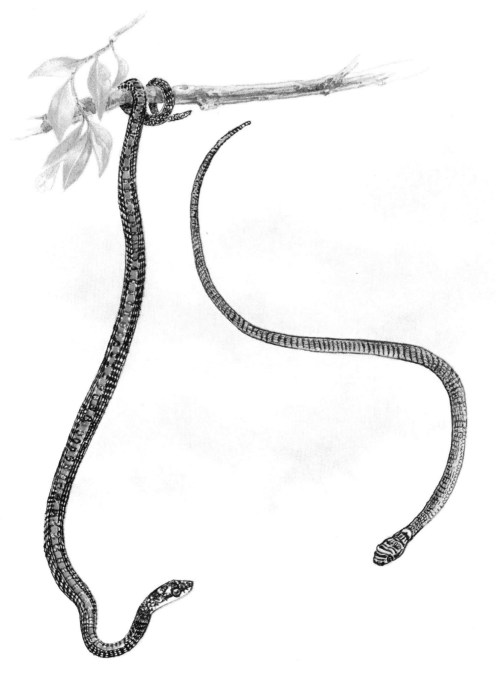

There are snakes
that hang, then glide.

Scaly skin is rough

or soft.

When it's old,
it peels right off.

Snakes with fangs—

a scary sight.

Snakes with fangs
have poison bites!

Snakes that
coil small.

Snakes that
stretch tall.

Round and thick snakes.

Thin-like-sticks snakes.

Snakes with flat snouts.

Forked tongues flick out.

Snake eggs.

One snake.

Two snakes.

Three.

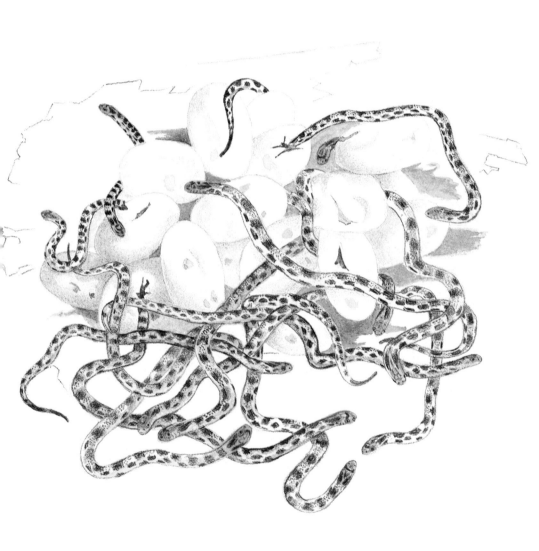

Now how many
do you see?

Snakes eat bugs and
rats and fish.

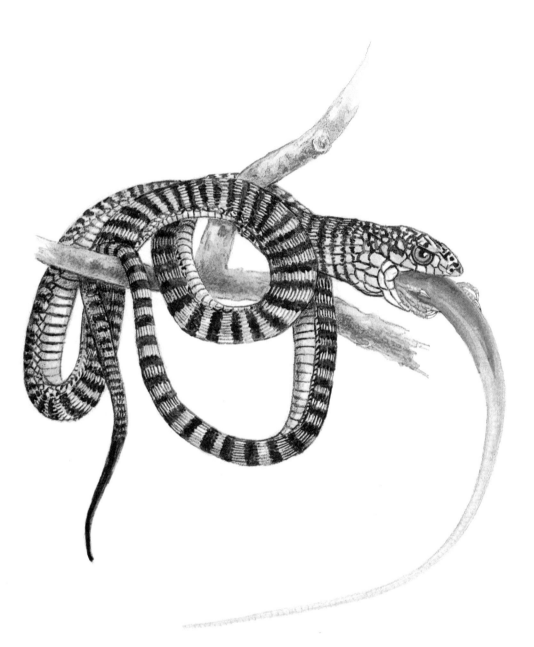

A lizard makes a
tasty dish.

Chickens, frogs, and,
for a treat, a crocodile—

that's quite a feat!

Snakes with rattles.

Snakes in battles.

Snakes that play dead.

Snakes with two heads.

Two snakes.

Four snakes.

Six snakes.

Eight.
Every single
snake is great!

Cover:
Red Diamond
Rattlesnake

Page 3:
Indian Cobras

Page 4:
Eastern Garter Snake

Page 4:
Red-sided
Garter Snake

Page 4:
Smooth Green Snake

Page 4:
Rosy Boa

Page 5:
Spotted Leaf-nosed
Snake

Page 5:
Sand Snake

Page 5:
Blue Racer

Page 5:
Hognose Snake

Page 6:
Diamondback
Rattlesnake

Page 6:
Coral Snake

Page 7:
Carpet Python

Page 7:
Corn Snake

Page 8:
Saw-scaled Viper

Page 8:
Emerald Tree Boa

Page 9:
Mountain Kingsnake

Page 9:
Banded Sea Krait

Page 10:
Yellow Rat
Snake

Page 10:
Mud Snake

Page 11:
Flying Snakes

Page 12:
Rough-scaled
Tree Viper

Page 13:
Black Racer

Page 14:
Copperhead Snake

Page 15:
Gaboon Viper

Page 16:
Pit Viper

Page 16:
Cobra

Page 17:
Cottonmouth

Page 17:
Thread Snake

Page 18:
Hognose Snake

Page 18:
Python

Page 21:
Fox Snakes

31

Page 22:
Yellow Rat Snake

Page 23:
Boomslang

Pages 24-25:
Anaconda

Page 26:
Pygmy Rattlesnake

Page 26:
Sand Vipers

Page 27:
Grass Snake

Page 27:
Two-headed
Gopher Snake

Page 28:
Blind Snake

Page 28:
Sonora Whipsnake

Page 28:
Western Ribbon Snake

Page 28:
Kirtland's Water Snake

Page 29:
Common Kingsnake

Page 29:
Ground Snake

Page 29:
Night Snake

Page 29:
Sidewinder